101 Creepy, Weird, Scary, Interesting, and Outright Cool Facts

A collection of 101 facts that are sure to leave you creeped out and entertained at the same time.

Table of Contents

Introduction

"Teach me something I don't know!" is something we commonly hear our readers say, or at least think. Indeed, one of the most powerful driving forces behind our random browsing the Internet (or a local library) is the pursuit of new information.

And sometimes, just sometimes, this new information can be completely random – *we just want something new*. Whether we are looking for new trivia about our favorite celebrities and TV stars, some new, juicy technological info, or an obscure historical fact, we want it.

Sometimes the information we are looking for shocks us in a certain way – if, for example, we learned that our favorite actor starring in a new vampire movie is indeed a vampire, we would be at least interested what is behind the story. And if we learn that his girlfriend was found dead last week, without a single drop of blood in her veins, we would be legitimately creeped out – regardless of whether the story we read is true, or not.

Which brings us to one of the goals of this little book. Our goal is first and foremost to entertain you, along with teaching you some new things you did not know before. On top of that, we aim to provide you some pretty scary information. If you read through the whole book and never get even slightly worried about what you find, then congratulations – you are a very brave and calm person. But eventually, you will acquire some new conversation fuel for the next Halloween party.

The book is divided into several categories, in order to let you find the topic you are most interested in as easy as possible – although you are encouraged to read what looks most interesting first, be sure that you will find entertaining stuff all over.

There is a well-known quote circling around the Internet, in various versions and interpretations. One of the versions shows a picture of Abraham Lincoln beside it, while the quote says:

"The worst thing about the Internet is that you can never be sure what you just read was true or not." --Albert Einstein

The notable sarcasm in the quote is twofold – neither was the Internet around at the time when Einstein (let alone Lincoln) was alive, nor is the person on the picture Einstein at all. With that in mind, we aimed to provide a comprehensive list of actual *facts* for you – not just random rumors, but the information we made sure is correct, by checking out various references and literature. In the final chapter of this book you will even find some short urban legends – all of which were confirmed to be true. Not only that – throughout the book we even included a few other factoids, which turned out to be false, and debunked them – showing that the true side of the story is just as terrifying, if not even more.

All in all, it is our sincerest hope that you will find out some new things. And that those new things will scare you. And just as importantly, provide entertainment.

So without further ado, let's get to the facts!

PLANTS AND ANIMALS

1.   A tree grew in the Sahara desert.

The Tree of Ténéré in Niger was once considered to be the most solitary tree ever to grow. It was an acacia tree, which grew over 250 miles (400 km) away from any other patch of plants, surface water source or any other piece of living nature, let alone civilization.

In the local culture it was considered a sacred tree, its very existence being a little mystery of its own. Evidently, the tree that stood around 10 feet (over 3 m) tall, had rooted so deep into the ground to catch a table of underground water *around 115 feet (35 m) below the surface.*

Tragically, *in 1973, a drunk truck driver crashed into it,* breaking down the famous landmark tree. The tree was preserved and moved to the Niger National Museum, while a metal sculpture was put in its place.

2.   A sea cucumber will vomit its intestines when threatened.

Sea cucumbers are a class of invertebrate marine animals which inhabit almost every sea in the world. Their bodies can regenerate at an exceptionally fast rate, which allows them to regrow organs that were completely lost. As such, they have developed a defensive mechanism where they throw out their intestines – and sometimes even more internal organs – when they are attacked by predators.

3. Vampire bats rarely bite humans.

Unlike vampires from our beloved horror stories, vampire bats prefer biting larger, more peaceful animals such as cattle and horses. Their bites are completely harmless, though – so don't worry about being turned into a vampire or a ghoul. The only risk they carry is the disease called rabies, which they are immune to, but may carry over to other animals. Indeed, there were successful extractions of rabies serum from vampire bats.

4. Kakapo – critically endangered, but why?

Australia is home to some of the most bizarre and fascinating creatures that live today. One of them is a parrot species called kakapo. Kakapo is one of the largest parrot species, and is sometimes called an "owl parrot", due to its nocturnal nature.

The species is critically endangered, counting less than 150 living specimens in the wild. Strangely enough, this endangerment has little to do with humans this time. Kakapo is a flightless bird, and due to its bulky mass is not among the fastest runners. On top of all that, the kakapo has a strong body odor which is very pleasant and therefore can be easily located by the predators. As such, its numbers are being thinned by other predators – whose numbers are another thing Australia can boast with.

5. A polar bear's liver is poisonous – by vitamins.

In various cultures, pork or chicken liver is considered a delicacy, due to its taste and nutritious value. The same is true for liver of some wild animals, such as boars or deer. However, eating a polar bear's liver will most likely kill an average human – but not due to its poison.

Polar bears have liver that is rich in vitamin A, containing 24,000 – 35,0000 IU (international units) per gram. For humans, a tolerable upper limit is 10,000 IU, while doubling this amount will result in first symptoms of hypervitaminosis (vitamin toxicity). Tripling the amount, which is normal for polar bears (who are immune to such hypervitaminosis), would result in death.

6. The Grolar bear

There is an ongoing debate of how much influence mankind has on the global warming, but one thing is clear – global warming is real, and it is a danger not only to humans, but to many plants and animals as well. Among the endangered ones are polar bears who, in search for food, have started migrating south from their natural habitat.

Consequently, this led them to encounters with brown bears, and such encounters were not as violent as we might think at first – in fact, the polar bears have successfully *mated* with brown bears and grizzlies, spawning a beastly legacy which is nowadays nicknamed *grolar bears*. This is not cryptozoology, however – the specimens have indeed been caught and observed. These hybrids display traits of both species, being larger than an average grizzly (although smaller than a polar bear), and can be as aggressive and intelligent as either of those.

7.   The monstrous rats of Tehran

In Tehran, Iran, a squad of snipers is employed to protect citizens from – rats! Do not think for a single moment that such rats could be easily dealt with by a domestic cat, because the poor cat may this time end up having its rear side kicked big time.

The official statement is that the rats were exposed to radiation, which resulted in a severe genetic mutation. They now grow up to over 5 kilograms (10 pounds), and are just as cunning, aggressive and always hungry as the small sewer rats we have all seen. Although there is a disagreement to their origins within the scientific community, there is really no evidence that would point to an explanation where the ravenous, overgrown rodents came from. Good thing they are not skilled in the far-eastern martial arts... we hope.

8.   The "incompetent" jaws of a crocodile

Crocodiles are one of the most fearsome predators on land – they cause a good number of annual human and livestock deaths, as well as hunting wild prey – in fact, they will eat just about anything that comes too close a swamp, river or lake they call home.

However, much like some other reptiles, crocodiles do not chew their food. In fact, their teeth are almost ornamental – they swallow their food whole, and their powerful bite is strong enough to simply *crush* through nearly any piece of flesh and bone. On top of that, they are unable to stick their tongues out.

9.   Komodo dragon's mouth is cleaner than our own

We all heard rumors and tell-tales about a dog's mouth containing less bacteria and other microbes than humans'. We also heard a myth about the Komodo dragon having a fatally "dirty" mouth – its bite was said to kill the victim through *infection*, rather than venom.

This is one of the myths that people accept because "it's just too awesome to be false" - but sadly, it *is* false indeed. A study in 2013 showed no exceptional "cocktail" of infections in the animal's mouth – and in fact, it showed even less bacteria than in most mammals, humans included.

So what gives? The Komodo dragon in fact does have venom glands. For obvious reasons, those were not researched well enough until recently, and the venom does work similar to some diseases – it kills the prey slowly. Combined with the animal's exceptional perception of scent, it is indeed able to bite you, and then follow you patiently until you die, before eating you in peace.

10. Immortal jellyfish

Turritopsis dohrnii, as known among biologists, is one of the very few species known to be immortal. It is a species of jellyfish which, after having reached sexual maturity, can revert to a completely immature state.

Imagine transforming into a completely healthy toddler right after you grow too old to have children – this is exactly what those jellyfish do.

The scary part is that they can still multiply, and there are few known predators and diseases which can end their lives "prematurely". Therefore, one day they may take over the world.

11. Fish with human teeth

The Sheepshead Bay in Brooklyn, New York City, was named after an infamous, ravenous species of fish which barely even lives there.

The fish is notorious for feeding on clams, crabs, mussels, sand fleas – essentially, just about *anything which features a hard shell*. The most bizarre part is that their teeth have evolved specifically for breaking those shells – and they strangely resemble *human teeth*.

To make things even more bizarre, they are classified as whitefish, which means catching them in a net is downright impossible – you need a hook and a bait. Known as bait-stealers, they require a rather small hook to be caught.

Smile!

12. The magnificent blue whale

Blue whales are the largest known animals ever to exist. That is right, they are larger than any discovered dinosaur ever was.

To put things into perspective, a *blue whale's tongue can weigh as much as an elephant*, while their heart can weigh as much as a personal car. Its heart is so large, that *a grown human can swim through its arteries*. To make this even more interesting, a blue whale's mass is so large, that it cannot survive on land. If a blue whale would be put out of the ocean, it would crush under its own weight. The ocean carries its respective weight.

On top of everything – *blue whales are carnivores*. Luckily, they only feed on tiny species of fish and crabs, called *plankton*. They filter around five tons of water with each mouthful, and eat over three and a half tons of plankton on a daily basis.

13. Insects, bats, light and vampires

It is known that bats, although almost blind, are drawn to light sources. The reason for this is simple – they know they will find delicious bugs there.

However, why are insects drawn towards light? Surprisingly – nobody knows. If you ever decide to study entomology, discovering the reason for this may earn you a doctorate.

It is also a known myth that garlic repels vampires. While we have never seen a vampire in real life, one thing is known – the smell of garlic does repel mosquitoes. Close enough, right?

14. Spiders and some insects do not have teeth.

Insects usually have two out of four possible mouth configurations – adapted for licking, sucking, stinging and biting or chewing. This means that some insects, such as flies, can never chew their food.

The same is true for most spiders.

So how are those animals able to eat anything larger than their mouths? Believe it or not, they vomit a highly reactive chemical over their food, making the insides melt into a thick liquid muss. The insect or spider then sucks the substance in. This essentially means *their food is digested before they even eat it.*

15. There is a wasp that preys on tarantulas.

After reading the previous, do you think spiders sound scary? Worse is yet to come. There is a species of wasp living all over the world – Africa, Americas, Southeast Asia and Australia – which grows up to 2 inch (5 cm) long. Its prey are mostly tarantulas.

By the end of the mating season, this nightmare-fuel wasp attacks a tarantula from behind with its venomous stinger. The venom usually only paralyzes the spider, rather than killing it instantly, which is when the wasps vicious plan continues.

The wasp then digs a hole in the ground, placing the dying,

paralyzed tarantula into it, before laying eggs on the spider's body. The idea here is that *the tarantula's meat remains as fresh as possible by the time the young wasplings hatch* – which is why the venom does not kill it too soon.

16. The Earth is not completely round.

This might strike as an intuitive one – we know there are mountains, river canals, depressions, volcanoes and all other wonders all over the Earth's crust. But we are not talking about that here. In fact, all those "irregularities" can be ignored, taking the Earth's radius (almost 4,000 miles, or 6,750 km) into account. If we took a perfectly polished 1-meter-radius steel sphere and then carved a notch a single millimeter deep – *the Earth's surface would be more "cleanly polished" than that*. Take a pocket calculator and do the math.

However, *the shape of earth is not spherical*. Due to its magnetic fields on the North and South Pole, as well as the gravitational impact of the Moon and the Sun, the Earth's shape is nowadays described as a *spheroid* – it is substantially "wider" than it is "tall".

17. Do you think you are standing still? Think again.

We cannot perceive the Earth's movement through space – and that is a good thing. The Earth rotates around its axes, and revolves around the Sun. And the speed at which it does so is pretty amazing.

If you were to stand on the Equator line, you would be *spinning at over 1,000 miles per hour* (1,650 km/h). The closer you get to either of the Poles, your rotational speed grows slower, until you would just be (theoretically) spinning around your own axis on the very Pole. But even so, at any given point, you would be *traveling through space at an amazing 67,000* (yes, sixty-seven *thousand*) *miles per hour* (almost 108,000 km/h)!

18. Compared to other planets, the Earth is very much alive.

We don't just mean the living creatures – plants, animals and such. Not even the microorganisms, like viruses and bacteria. We mean, *the very planet changes all the time.* Volcanoes spit out fresh magma every time they erupt – which is the seething-hot mass from underneath the Earth's crust. The crust, on the other hand gets drowned in this magma, and gets pushed to lower layers as the magma cools and dries down, only to be heated up again and spat out through volcanoes once more.

On top of that, this process, along with the magnetic fields on the Poles, makes the *entire liquid underground mass move around all the time* – which is one of the main reasons why the tectonic plates also move around. So even relatively speaking, you are *never* standing still – you are "sailing" on the plate of Earth's crust which floats all around.

Very slowly, though, *but it does move.*

19. Not even the magnetic poles are static axes.

In a few thousand years (hopefully), your compass will not move.

That's right – the magnetic poles of the Earth will completely disappear, as they have a lot of times in the past. Not only that, but *when they reappear they will switch places.*

This is a phenomena called *paleomagnetism*, which occurs every few thousand (up to million) years. Currently, the poles are moving at roughly 8 – 12 miles (15 km) per year. Not much, until we see the consequences.

As if this was not weird enough, consequences are the really scary part – the Earth's magnetic field is one of the most powerful forces that protects us from dangerous cosmic radiation, especially from the Sun. It has been shown by geologists that *this is one of the main reasons for global warming – and there is absolutely nothing we can do about it.*

20. Walking rocks

A rock going out for an evening walk sounds rather silly, until you catch one doing exactly that. Well, they don't have legs, so it should be better called "slide" – but you get the picture.

There is a valley where, during nighttime, when temperature turning causes strong gusts of wind, and humidity turns into frost on the smooth ground surface – as well as rocks – the friction between rocks and the ground gets so low, that the wind carries rocks around for several miles.

The valley is called the Death valley.

21.   The deadliest place on Earth

One of the most beautiful crystal caves on Earth is Cueva de los Cristales, in Mexico. But it is as deadly as it is beautiful. No, there is no poisonous gas in those caves, nor is there any beast that would hunt you down.

In fact, there is almost *nothing* alive in those caves, due to the combination of air pressure, humidity and temperature. The humidity is exactly 100%, while the temperature is (near the entrance) around 122°F (50°C).

Why is this a deadly combination? Because it essentially means the air is full of vaporous water, and *the coolest place around are your own lungs.* So as soon as you breathe in, the vapor decides to turn into water inside your lungs which, combined with the said temperature causes your body to fail rapidly.

22.   The coldest places on Earth

It might come as no surprise that the coldest place on Earth is Antarctica – but how cold is it? The Russian Antarctic research station Vostok had a struggle measuring the temperature. Allegedly, the coldest month in Antarctica is August, where the temperature went almost as low as -90°c (-130°F). This is not the record cold, but the "most reliable measurement", since *the extreme cold caused many instruments to malfunction.*

The runner-up for this competition is Oymaykon in Russia, where the lowest temperature measured was "only" -71.2°C (-96.2°F). The main difference here is around 20°C (35°F), but there is also one other notable distinction – *Oymaykon is permanently inhabited*, i.e. it is an actual settlement, where people reside.

23. The Dark castles and catacombs of Hell

This name sounds like a good title for one or two horror films, or for some heavy metal or shock rock albums. In fact, it is one of the most popular tourist attractions in Iceland.

Called the "Dimmuborgir" in Iceland and Scandinavia (after which a well-known Norwegian extreme metal bands got their name), this massive complex indeed strangely resembles the ruins of some old castle. In the Icelandic and Scandinavian folklore it is considered to be the gateway to Hell, while in the Norse Christian folklore they went as far as claiming this is the exact place where Satan himself fell from Heaven, and underneath which he built the catacombs of Hell ("Helvetes katakomber" in Norse).

The really scary part? *This whole complex is natural.* It is clearly a lava rock formation, which could have not been constructed by man.

24. The horror of Antarctica

There is another thing you should know about Antarctica, which is far scarier than the one mentioned above. The continent is frozen under many *layers of ice*, which geologists and meteorologists observe to study how it developed during the past millions of years.

This ice – which is in some places over 3 miles (4 km) thick – is a wealth of freshwater. In fact, it contains roughly 70% of the planet's freshwater. Not only that – evidence shows that *there is no less than 200 lakes under the ice* – which are still in liquid, freshwater form.

But the scary part here is that *this freshwater is slowly cutting loose*. Due to global warming, there is a *net loss* in the mass of the ice caps. If all the ice of Antarctica would melt, not only would the salt level in oceans significantly drop (causing mass extinction of saltwater creatures), but *it would also raise the global sea level by 200 feet* (almost 61 m).

25. The frosty bloom

The Arctic circle is not as nearly scary as Antarctica, but this might be due to the fact that it is better explored. There are still some weird phenomena there.

One of them is a blossom of flower-snowflake hybrid structures which sometimes appears on the sea surface. Since saltwater freezes at much lower temperatures than freshwater, the ice does not form as easily, but when it does, it stays there and keeps growing, as long as the air temperature is below zero.

The so-called frost flowers appear to be straight out of an alien-themed Sci-Fi film. When a tiny speck of dirt (or any other solid substance) flows on the surface long enough, ice starts forming around it – but it does not resemble an iceberg. Instead, a crystalline structure forms around it, much like a snowflake, which can grow to the size and shape of a large flower – *amazingly beautiful, but deadly cold.*

26. *The call of the Cthulhu*

In 1997, near Antarctica, one of the most mysterious sounds ever was caught by the National Oceanic and Atmospheric Administration. It was an extremely deep and powerful sound wave, with the frequency ranging from 0 to 50 Hz within roughly a minute. Moreover, *it was so loud it could be heard within the radius of over 3,100 miles* (5,000 km).

The researchers, as well as the news reporters, were unsure what the source of this sound – nicknamed "The Bloop" – was. There were theories which credited the sound to a marine life-form (hopefully animal, and not alien), while others claimed it was the sound of two huge icebergs sliding against each other. Some even went so far as to claim it was the sound of the legendary Cthulhu, from H.P. Lovecraft's mythos, finally awakening.

Eventually the mystery was resolved by providing similar recordings, all of underwater icequakes – this was merely a very large one which quickly gained in popularity. Yet, an iceberg large enough to make a sound of that power is now probably still floating freely – and *it is many times larger than the one which sank the Titanic.*

27. Church websites are, on average, more often infected by viruses than any other.

Church websites – especially from smaller, local churches – are often ran and maintained by volunteers. Usually it is a single volunteer doing it in their free time, rather than a trained, and highly experienced professional who does it for a living. As such, security breaches in such websites are not as likely to be detected in time, let alone resolved.

28. By throwing away your phone, you are essentially discarding gold.

There is a small amount of precious metals in all e-waste – mobile phones (*not* just smartphones), desktop, laptop and tablet PCs – virtually every little piece of electronics.

Gold is one of the best electric conductors available, and when put inside an isolated environment (such as inside a chip), it provides the highest quality electronic backbone for decades – perhaps even centuries. Throughout the world, there is a (small) number of industries which make a fortune on harvesting gold and other precious metals from e-waste.

Around 2010, it was estimated that, in USA only, *there was around 60 million dollars worth in gold dumped in e-waste* – and this number shows a trend of rapid growth.

29. In 1982, Tron did not receive an Academy Award, due to computer use.

"Tron" is a cult-classic film from 1982, directed by Steven Lisberger and released by Buena Vista, under the production of Walt Disney Studios. It was, however, not nominated an Academy award for special effects, which were – to be honest – spectacular for their time. The Motion Picture Academy refused the nomination, according to Lisberger, due to the fact that they used computers in order to create special effects, and the Academy considered that "cheating". Good to know, since nowadays there is not a single Hollywood film without computer-generated special effects anymore.

30. The first Google server casing was built from LEGO bricks.

Sergey Brin and Larry Page, the masterminds behind the largest IT project in the world started out with little beyond a pile of budget PC components assembled – or, better to say, scrapped – together. In 1996, they had to assemble multiple components, such as ten hard disks, into working clusters, the expenses for such machinery left them without funds to buy a decent computer casing. Thus, they built the casing from LEGO building blocks. Two years later, it was superseded by a large production server rack. Then, two years after that, their computing power counted around 5,000 (yes, five thousand) computers, and today the number is estimated to between 1,5 and 2 million. Talk about investment and growth!

31. Are computers more powerful than the human brain?

An average modern home computer processor (in 2015) is able to perform roughly between 5 and 7 trillion mathematical operations per second. It is estimated the human brain does a lot more. If one day someone designs a computer processor able to perform around 30 – 40 quadrillion operations per second, this could theoretically compete with an average human brain. However, this fact alone is very unreliable. For example, if you can calculate a square root from a ten-digit number in less than a second – using your brain only – you are still slower than an average desktop computer. Try it yourself, on your PC. The main difference is that our brain is adapted to perform millions of operations *at the same time*, due to our constant perception and processing of information around us. Computers, on the other hand, are designed for performing complex mathematical operations quickly – *one at a time.*

32. The Dark Side of the Internet

There is a whole layer of the World Wide Web right under your fingertips, which you can never access through "conventional" means – it is not listed in search engines, the social media and the social bookmarking sites almost never mention it, and you are highly unlikely to stumble upon them just by surfing the Web.

The terms Dark Web, Deep Web, Invisible Web, etc. have been in use ever since the Web was around. Although Deep Web and Dark Web are not the same thing, most people mistakenly identify them for one and the same. The Invisible Web is a benevolent part of it, where website owners merely wish to avoid being indexed around. On the other hand, the Dark Web is a terrifyingly "evil" part of the Internet where people can engage in a widest variety of illegal activities – from purchasing illegal drugs and watching videos of other people performing violent crimes, all the way to hiring professional assassins. And no, we are not going to tell you how to get there – you are better off without it.

33. Most hackers are good guys.

When we say "hacker", the first thing that comes to mind is a nerdy guy in his garage or basement, staring at his computer for at least a few dozen hours straight, breaking into some computer network and making thousands – or millions – of dollars of damage.

Luckily, "hacker" is a much broader term. Some people do not even limit it to computer hacking.

By definition, a "hack" is *an intelligent solution to an interesting problem*", and most hackers are actually in it just for exploring. Through exploring, they find holes in computer systems, and most of them will report those holes and propose patches for them, rather than exploiting them for their own selfish goals. *The selfish ones are actually a minority*, while the majority of them are in fact the so-called *white-hat hackers*, who make a living from *preventing* disasters, rather than causing them.

And even hackers which deal with illegal activities are nowadays rather busy with harassing various hate groups, terrorist organizations and similar "movements" online.

34. Your cell phone is dirty. Very dirty.

Remember when doctors claimed our phones expose us to dangerous radiation? The truth is much worse. We rarely wash our hands before touching our phones. Also, our phones produce a bit of heat, and we keep them in warm places (such as our pockets), which helps germs grow. Then, very few of us clean our phones regularly with some kind of antiseptic.

Research has shown that an average cell phone is the home to roughly 25,000 (yes, twenty-five *thousand*) germs (i.e. not just "any kind" of bacteria – the *unsafe* ones). This number has grown in the past years due to the growing usage of touchscreens, whereas with classic phones it used to be a little bit smaller. The same is true for your tablet PC.

This essentially means that *an average cell phone contains up to eighteen times more germs than an average public restroom.*

Go clean your phone before you continue reading.

35. Pocket vibration hallucinations are real.

Have you ever "felt" your phone vibrate in your pocket (or on your table), only to find out it was only your imagination? If the answer is no, then you should consider yourself lucky.

There is a recognized condition among psychology experts, dubbed the "Phantom pocket vibration syndrome." Disturbingly, the number of people affected by it is at this moment only estimated – but the worst-case scenario statistics have shown *just slightly under 90% of young people, while around 50% the Generation X is estimated to be affected by it.*

While there is currently no clear scientific consensus on what exactly causes this kind of hallucinations, it is clear that it correlated with frequent cell phone usage. What is worse, *nobody knows what other disorders it may cause in the future.*

36. Nintendo was around before computers existed.

Nintendo, one of the most popular video game and gaming console manufacturers, is a Japanese company which has sold over half a billion hardware units and over 4 billion software units so far.

Here's the weird part – as noted in the title, it was around before home computers. In fact, *it existed before any kind of consumer electronics at all.* The company started in 1889 as a playing card manufacturer, which crafted handmade cards along with printed ones. *The playing card business still exists to this date* – and is still successful.

37. The World Wide Web grows quickly. Very quickly.

Have you ever tried visiting every single web site on the Internet? Do not even try.

Although it is probably easier than sending an e-mail to every single address in existence (since *e-mail was around before the WWW*), you will probably lose it before even managing to browse through one tenth of current web sites. Not web pages, web sites, i.e. just typing www.(something).com, rather than browsing through entire sitemaps.

The World Wide Web, as of early 2010s, grows at an almost disturbing rate – there are *more than one million web sites registered every month*.

Still thinking about visiting them all?

38. *The most expensive project ever*

Imagine, if you will the following nightmare – somebody imprisons you in a shopping mall with one billion dollars, which you must spend to the last penny before being let out.

If you somehow find a way to spend *$200 every minute, without sleeping*, you would manage to get out *in just a bit under 10 years*. Take a pocket calculator and check it yourself, if you do not believe it.

However, there was a project 150 times more expensive than that. It is the International Space Station (ISS), which *cost roughly 150 billion US dollars – so far*. The assembly of ISS started in 1990, and was assembled (mostly) into its current state in 2011. That was 21 years to spend $150 billion – or, on average, *$13,5 thousand every minute*.

39. *Filthy stinking rich*

This is the phrase that would most accurately describe the drug lord Pablo Emilio Escobar Gaviria, arguably the wealthiest criminal in known history. Not only that – at his peak, he was in the top 10 of world's richest people. At that time, he was in control of roughly 80% of the cocaine smuggled into the USA.

His wealth, since it was earned illegally, is difficult to pinpoint – but the rough estimations are mind-blowing at least. In early 1990s (not long before his death in 1993), his net worth was *estimated between $30 billion and $100 billion, the later taking into account all the cash he had secretly stashed* throughout his Columbia, his homeland.

Here comes the most "filthy stinking" part, though – since most of his money was stashed in difficult-to-find (yet not so clean) places, it was estimated that *$1 billion of his money was eaten by rats every year.*

40.   *War against poverty, not poor people.*

This may sound like a slogan for some political party, or a prosperous, fast-growing industry, but it is in fact one of the main goals of modern economic research.

Only in the USA, by 2015, *there have been over 80 anti-poverty programs presented*, all of which were means-tested, i.e. they could theoretically work if put in place. Due to various political and economic complications, some of them have shown to be unsuccessful – many rich individuals and organizations are unwilling to cooperate, while the poor want things to develop faster.

The worst part of this is, there are new anti-poverty programs emerging on an annual basis – and *almost none of them are even tried out in practice.*

41. Ponder this before robbing a bank.

There are, on average, between 20 and 30 bank robberies worldwide. Most incidents evidently involve more than a single culprit, which means the "loot" needs to be divided among the robbers who took part in it.

But let us assume every successful robbery involved a single person. After four attempted robberies within a single year – *at most* – every bank robber is caught. This is not a statistically calculated probability, it is a hard number which the Western law enforcements boast with.

Assuming those four attempts were successful, a bank robber will "earn" less than 20,000 American dollars (or 13,000 British pounds). This is just slightly above a minimum annual UK wage, and around 33% higher than a minimum annual US wage. However, *it is far below half of average annual UK or US wage.* Let us repeat that these numbers mean something only if you rob the bank alone.

So, before you attempt a life of crime, consider getting a job instead.

42. 92% of the world's currency exists in computers only.

Yes, ninety-two percent. If your bank account currently holds $100, it means that only $8 of it actually exists in cash – everything else is virtual currency. If all the world's computers would suddenly break tonight, an average person would be left with no more than eight percent of their current wealth. It gets worse than that – the richer you are, the more of your actual money is held in such bank accounts and similar virtual places, while the less wealthy people hold a larger percentage of their monetary property in physical cash, stashed somewhere home. This means that a total computer (and actually, just Internet) breakdown would mean the fastest "rich vs. poor" revolution ever.

43. How much does it cost to make a dollar?

American dollars, like all printed money, start out as pieces of paper and ink used to print the value on them. Printing money is a complex process, which uses special paper and ink, along with a number of security measures which prevent conunterfeiting.

Taking mass production into account, and the fact that nobody will ever print a *single* dollar bill, but a large number of them in a bulk, the printing price may come up surprisingly cheap.

It costs less than 10 cents to print a $1 bill. A mere 10 cents per dollar bill is enough to cover the industry expenses. To make things weirder, making coins is much more expensive – forging a penny costs just a bit under $0.025 (2.5 cents). A real bargain is, of course a $100 bill – it costs exactly the same as a $1 bill.

44. Paper money is not paper.

Take a piece of paper and print (or just write) something on it. Now fold it a few times, place it in your hind pocket, sit on it, take it out, fold and re-fold it some more. How long do you think this piece of paper will last? Will it live up to a month, or even a year? How much do you think will it take before it becomes illegible?

In order to make American Dollars last longer, they are printed on cloth, rather than paper. *75% of a dollar bill is cotton, while 25% is linen.* This cloth mixture is far more durable than plain paper – life expectancy of an average $1 bill is almost six years. On the other hand, an average $100 bill can live up to 15 years.

45. Mt. Money

Every year, a certain number of dollar bills is re-printed, in order to replace destroyed and worn-out bills. The bills which are no longer usable are recycled, and were burned in the past. But how much exactly is destroyed?

In 2012, a total amount of over $350 billion was *returned* into circulation – this does not account for *new* bills that were put in that year. To put that into perspective, let us check the next little bit of info.

By the end of the 20th century, if you gathered all the worn-out $1 bills and stacked them one above the other, *it would peak up to over 65 miles* (105 km). And Mount Everest is only 5.5 miles (8.85 km) tall!

46. Who earns the most?

There is a good number of very prosperous industries in the

Western world, all of which count billions of American dollars in annual earnings.

Of course, here we will not take illegal activities into account – if commerce such as the production, distribution and enjoyment of hallucinogenic drugs was legal, it would ruin the economy for most manufacturers and distributors, because they would be forced to pay humongous taxes.

However, only in USA, we can look at the film industry, sports, music distribution, theme parks, and so on. And there is a legal industry in the USA which generates more revenue than *all the aforementioned together*. It is called *gambling* – and it generates over $40 billion per year.

47.   The worst inflation ever

Luckily, this belongs to history as much as it belongs into economics – but nevertheless, it is a disturbing fact to think about.

By "worst inflation," we mean relatively here – there were countries in history with worse inflation than the following one, but none has fallen from one of the top Western industries down to such poverty in such a short time. Of course, we are talking about the post-World War I Germany.

In 1923, the German currency (*Deutsche Mark*) has lost so much of its value that it was virtually worthless – money was given to children to play, used as wallpaper, even burning paper (being cheaper than wooden spills, let alone coal). *If you wanted to buy a loaf of bread on the market, you would literally have to carry a full wheelbarrow of money.*

48.   *There is a fear for nearly everything.*

Sure, there is *acrophobia* (fear of high places), *agoraphobia* (fear of open spaces), *claustrophobia* (fear of closed spaces), as well as *homophobia* and *xenophobia* (both essentially meaning "being a bad person", rather than some actual fear).

However, did you know that *George Washington suffered from taphephobia* (fear of being buried alive)? *Richard Nixon, on the other hand, had nosocomephobia* (he was afraid of hospitals), while *Napoleon Bonaparte suffered from ailurophobia* (irrational fear of cats).

Comedian Woody Allen might be the most peculiar of all – he suffers from *panophobia*, which is *fear of virtually everything.* Heights, bright colors, insects, elevators, closed spaces... you name it, mr. Allen is afraid of it – or at least was at one time. He is under psychoanalysis since 1970s.

And since we're talking about psychoanalysis, none other than *Sigmund Freud was supposedly afraid of ferns.*

49. *Nylon tights, stilettos and wigs used to be macho.*

If we skip the Middle Ages (where the situation was not all too different in the East), the fashion statements throughout history differed from those of our time greatly. Nowadays, especially in the Western world, high heels and tights are most commonly associated with women – usually even considered very womanly and seductive. A wig, on the other hand, is somewhat of a taboo topic, but it is known to be worn by both men and women who are unhappy with their own hair (or lack thereof).

However, *the first wearers of such apparel were men*. While the tradition of wearing high heels dates as early as the 9th century Persia (again, by men), the fashion craze for it began in the 16th century Europe. It went as far as both tights and high heels being *a symbol of masculinity*, while *wigs were exclusive to noble men*. Grab a history book and take a look at the portrait of, e.g. King Louis XIV – a true macho for his time.

50. Napoleon Bonaparte was not short.

There is a widespread rumor that Napoleon was a short man – some would even claim terms like a "dwarf" or a "midget". There is even a psychological condition called "Napoleon Complex" which, contrary to the popular belief, does not mean the patient is deluded into thinking he is Napoleon – the more accurate name, in fact, would be the "Short Man Syndrome". The former is actually called the "Grandiose delusion". Imagine that.

In any case, Napoleon's recorded height was no less than 5 feet 7 inches (around 170 cm). The confusion here most likely emerged from two facts – first, this number is taken out of context. For his time and place, *Napoleon was of average to above average tall*.

Secondly, *he insisted on having his royal guard consist of tall men.* So, not only did he suffer from complexes due to his height – he insisted that his personal guards should be *even taller*. This is why he is, on numerous paintings, depicted as shorter – while the guards were in fact giants for their historical and geographical context.

51. Gold from the sea

There is something in old pirate legends – but we are not talking about gold coins and jewelery that was sunken during naval accidents or raids. There are tiny, microscopic grains of gold floating in the ocean – in fact, there is enough gold diluted in the oceans to make every person in the world moderately wealthy. (In such a case gold would become worthless, though.)

However, after the World War I, a German engineer by the name of Fritz Haber planned to exploit just that fact in order to help return the German war debt. He constructed a *machine which would extract gold dust from seawater* through a process called *electrolysis*, and mounted it on a ship. While initially successful – extracting over 60 milligrams of gold from a ton of seawater – he later on found a mistake in his calculations. The machine ended up extracting less gold than its initial and maintenance cost, making the whole project a failure.

52.   The original tooth fairy

We all know the tradition of storing lost baby teeth under a pillow, so that when a tooth fairy comes around, she would collect them and leave a small present for the child.

However, the tradition originates from Scandinavia, and is a little more creepy than a modern one. In Scandinavia, the *tooth fairy was in fact a plain witch*. Adults would hide their children's lost baby teeth, usually *burning* them. Why? Well, because if the witch finds a lost tooth, she could use it to cast a curse on a child.

Somehow we find the modern Western tradition a bit more appropriate.

53.   The Egyptian pyramids are extremely old.

We know that one, right? But it is difficult to put their age into perspective, without comparing them to some other historical events.

The first pyramids are estimated to date from he 27th century BCE, i.e. around 5,600 – 5,700 years ago. The last Egyptian pharao, Cleopatra VII Philopator (or just Cleopatra for short), died around the year 30 BCE – no more than 2050 years ago. This means that, chronologically, *Cleopatra was closer to our era than to the pyramids*.

But it gets even weirder. The last population of wooly mammoth, an extinct relative of the modern elephant, was found to be still alive some 4,000 years ago. Not only was the first pyramid finished while these animals were still very much alive – *they were contemporaries of the great pyramid of Giza.*

54. The first anti-smoking campaign

Here is a controversial one. Smoking was first questioned for its effect on human health during 1960s, around half a century after it became a "popular" habit in the Western world. However, the first powerful anti-smoking campaign in history dates two to three decades prior to this.

Between 1930 and 1940, a campaign was run in order to lower the tobacco consumption among citizens in Europe. The campaign had limited success, and had no legal bans on smoking, except among military and public servants.

The campaign originated in Germany, and was led by Adolf Hitler.

55. Madame Tussaud's carnival of death masks

The famous museum of wax figures in London, England, UK called *Madame Tussaud's* is one of your likely destinations if you ever visit this wonderful big city. And rightfully so – the wax figures are so lifelike, it is not often easy to tell they are not alive (apart from, you know, not moving). But how did it all come to be?

Marie Tussaud was a French noblewoman talented in the wax works who, like many other, was taught about the Revolution and encouraged to take her craft to the executions. Thus, she decided to start making lifelike and life-sized figures of executed individuals – the more popular, the better. She would take a severed head and dip it into melted wax, in order to make a "death mask". Once she reached the Great Britain, she toured with her death masks for over 30 years, before founding the museum.

56. True horror film stories

There is a number of horrific urban myths and legends floating around, but some of them were actually pulled straight out of historical records.

In the 15th-16th century United Kingdom, a man named Sawney Bean had a family of fifteen(!), who allegedly murdered over 1,000 people. In a similar, a bit older, record, Christie Cleek was a serial killer living somewhere in the hills. Both of them were supposedly cannibals, and were eventually captured and brought to justice.

Horror films like "The Hills Have Eyes" and "The Texas Chainsaw Massacre" were loosely based on records like these. However, modern historians are unsure of whether either of those men actually existed. Some argue one story is based on the other, while others argue *both stories might be based on true events.*

57. Shrunken heads

Some of the better-known South American (especially Amazonian) tribes acquired their fame through a skill of shrinking heads of their slain enemies. The process requires materials, time and skill – and, of course, an intact head of an enemy. Once the shrunken head is complete, *it is commonly used for decoration*, especially by the 19th century "civilized" people.

Indeed, the most disturbing part of this story is that the "civilized" folks would willingly trade with the said tribes for shrunken heads – providing them with firearms in exchange. The supply of firearms and ammunition did a decent job at providing more shrunken heads in return.

58. The shortest war in history

On 27 August 1896 the Anglo-Zanzibar war started. Two days earlier, the pro-British Sultan Hamad bin Thuwaini had died, and was succeeded by Sultan Khalid bin Barghash. The British demanded Barghash to leave the palace, in favor of Hamud bin Muhammed, another pro-British candidate.

Muhammed refused, to which the British declared war. Relatively speaking, the war casualties were terrible – a single British sailor was injured, while Zanzibar counted around 500 casualties. Taking into account that *the war lasted for no more than 38 minutes*, the density of the casualties can be compared to World War 1.

59. We eat insects on a daily basis.

Sure, there are cultures where insects are either presented as a delicacy, especially to rich tourists. There are also cultures where insects are one of the most important source of vital nutrients, such as proteins.

But would you believe you eat insects even in the Western culture? Evidently, there is no 100% certain way to remove insects out of natural foods, such as meat – especially ground meat – and vegetables. Most of these foods were insect-infested even before they were harvested, and the FDA (Food and Drug Administration in the United States of America) allows a certain portion of insects in every single food product. For example, it is allowed to have up to 60 insect parts (leg bits, wing parts, etc.) in 100 grams of chocolate!

On average, *a person living in the Western world eats between 400 and 450 whole insects per year* – which is around 1.1 – 1.25 insects daily. This would go a long way to explain why some foods have a certain crunchy quality to them.

60. Does 1+1=2 need proof? The answer is yes.

Evidently, it is not enough for some things to be "just plain obvious". Exact scientific disciplines, such as mathematics, physics, chemistry, biology etc. require solid proof for claims which are made, and only then can they be considered "facts" or "scientific theories" - otherwise, they are just called "hypotheses", and can be both proven and disproven.

Such is the example of the statement that one plus one equals two. The three-volume book titled *Principia Mathematica*, written by Alfred North Whitehead and Bertrand Russel, dedicates no less than 162 pages to the proof of this statement. Until then, "1+1=2" was considered an *axiom* in mathematics, a fact which cannot be proven, but has practical application, it is "obvious" to see, and its assumption "makes sense with everything else we know".

61.   Number forty is in alphabetical order.

Mathematics is considered to be one of the universal languages, especially among scientists and philosophers. Romans used letters to present numbers – for example, I is equivalent to one, V is five, X is ten, L is fifty, C is one hundred, D is five hundred and M is one thousand. In modern mathematics, numbers are represented in Arabic numerals (1, 2, 3, and so on), along with letters from both Latin and Greek alphabet.

Alongside with numerals, every number can be – in texts, rather than mathematical expressions – represented by a word. Thus, we have "one", "two", "three", "ten", "twenty", "hundred", "thousand", and so on. Interestingly enough, the number *forty* is the only one in English language whose letters are arranged in alphabetical order. No other number shares this feature in the English language, and very few Western languages have more than one such number. Here is a project for a rainy day – try finding another such number in your language.

62. *Upside-down years*

1961 was the last year so far which, when the number is turned upside-down, has the same value. Try writing 1961 on a piece of paper, then turn the paper upside-down – it will still be 1961. Another year like this was 1881, which was in the previous century. 1691, even earlier before that, was another "upside-down" year. So, a question needs to be asked – when will be the next such year? Taking the info above into account, it should not be long before another such year occurs, right?

Take a piece of paper again, and try out some combinations before you read on.

...would you believe, the next "upside-down" year will be 6009? Yes, once we are done with 1 being the first digit, it will take us quite a while before we reach another digit that actually has *any meaning whatsoever* when turned upside-down. So do not worry – we have a lot of time to prepare our conspiracy theories for the next one.

63. *There may be no such thing as "random".*

When we talk about "random", most of us can imagine rolling one or more dice, or shuffling a pack of cards in order to demonstrate the randomness. However, whether such patterns are really random or not, *it is virtually impossible to prove.*

Every "random" event we observe has its cause – the law of cause and effect, which we all know, demands that. However, once we dig into Heisenberg's uncertainty principle, as well as a little bit of quantum physics, we learn that *we can never fully determine the cause of an event.* We can measure things down to a "practically usable" level of detail, but every time we do, we inadvertently change the system we are observing.

Thus, we ourselves introduce a "random" level of "randomness" into every measurement we make, and following the previous rule, we are also unable to measure that!

If you think about this for too long, and your head does not start spinning, we recommend a career as a quantum physicist.

64. Are snowflakes exactly unique?

We are terribly sorry to burst anyone's bubble here. Seeing both claims numerous times (i.e. "every snowflake is unique" vs. "no snowflake is unique"), we feel this needs clarification. Also, the truth is far more interesting, let alone weird than you may think.

First of all, we do recognize 35 *basic snowflake shapes* today. But those are merely templates upon which actual snowflakes are built.

Secondly, it is clear that microscopic snowflakes and snow crystals (i.e. water crystals) *can* be identical. However, what we see with our bare eyes are *complex* snowflakes, which are composed of a large number of such crystals. Interestingly enough, those crystals grow in *fractals*, beautiful shapes described by complex mathematical functions.

But most mind-staggering part here is the *probability* of two snowflakes being identical. When we crunch the numbers on this, every complex snowflake can have one of many – *very* many – combinations. In fact, *the number of these combinations is larger than the total number of atoms in the known universe.* Thus, it is extremely unlikely you will see two identical snowflakes. Ever.

65. A duck's quack does not echo. Really?

Another myth that needs busting, mainly because the original claim was "A duck's quack doesn't echo, and nobody knows why." The reason why nobody knows why is because it is simply not true.

The truth is, it is very difficult to *hear* a duck's quack. But this has nothing to do with our hearing limitations. First of all, a duck's quack is rather quiet to begin with, and the echo can only be quieter than that (conservation of energy).

Secondly, the duck's quack starts out quiet, then gets a bit louder, and ends quiet again. In acoustics, it is called *fade in* and *fade out*. When such a sound echoes, it is difficult to perceive.

66. Coke could make you vomit.

We have all heard various claims and accusations thrown at Coca Cola, Pepsi, and other "cola" flavored soft drinks. One of the long-time favorites is that leaving a piece of liver in a glass of Coke through the night would make the tissue dissolve. The truth is, any soft drink *(including mineral water)* would do the job just as efficiently.

However, there is an ingredient in most Coke recipes which does nothing but prevent us from vomiting. Since these drinks usually contain ridiculous amounts of sugar (some close to, some over 100% of the recommended daily intake), which makes us crave for more of it, the manufacturers are forced to add phosphoric acid in order to neutralize the sweetness.

If Coke did not contain phosphoric (or some similar) acid, it would make us vomit from all the sugar we would suddenly receive.

67. Who says there is no water in outer space?

This is a quack we sometimes hear from people who have no knowledge of astronomy, chemistry of basic physics – some would call them "scientifically illiterate". And while there are those who then attempt to rescue themselves claiming "there is no water in liquid form out there", this is a failure too.

There is, however, a huge mass of water discovered in 2011, which contains over 100 trillion times more water than our planet, and 50 times more than its surrounding galaxy. It was first noticed in 1998 and identified as a quasar, but by now it has also been recognized as a *supermassive black hole*.

Luckily enough, it is 12 billion light years away from our planet. Still, it is terrifying to imagine – *the largest known water reservoir in the universe is a black hole.*

68. Black holes are far from static.

Unlike actual stars, which obediently revolve around their gravitational centers (like centers of their galaxies), thus appearing relatively static, black holes are under no such boundaries.

While they do not (usually!) bounce around space like in a gargantuan pinball machine, their gravitational fields allow them to escape the pull of most others. Taking their growing mass and virtually no friction into account, some have been measured to *hurl through space at an unbelievable 900 million miles per hour* (almost 1,500 million km/h). And yes, they *can change direction –* if they collide with an object whose mass is enough to make them "steer".

69. There are even planets which do not follow an orbit.

Called the *rogue planets*, these planets were at a certain point in their history either knocked out of their orbits – or never had one in the first place. The reasons for this are numerous, some of them being a collision with another object like themselves, or the proximity of a black hole (as mentioned above) – but the scary part is, they are now doing the same thing to other planets.

As they do not follow a certain orbit, and *they are usually at least the size and mass of Jupiter*, their gravitational fields allow them to change the course of any other planet they happen to fly by. And the scariest part of this story is – *there are more rogue planets in the universe than stars.*

So next time someone (other than your kid) asks you "how many stars are there in space?" feel free to answer "less than rogue planets," and give them a bit of nightmare fuel.

70. *Space is essentially infinite darkness. In every possible way.*

Space is beautiful – if you observe it from a safe place, like the surface of our own planet. The Earth has a wealth of bright light, warmth, pleasant sounds and smells and all the other things we, Earth people, take for granted.

Once you get in space, there is no light. Unless you are looking straight at a nearby star (like our Sun from the orbit of the Earth or Moon), you are looking into an incomprehensibly deep ocean of darkness, with just a few light bits here and there. And that is only if you are inside or relatively near a galaxy. Otherwise – pitch black.

But it does not stop there. The space is a vacuum, which means no sound. If you float around in a space suit, you can only hear your own breathing and perhaps your heartbeat. And your own voice, if you talk to yourself. Oh, and say goodbye to gravity – all your stuff will be scattered around, floating just like you. Since there is no gravity and no star to revolve around, you would soon lose track of time and space. Not to mention you would most surely die in space, without air, water, food or heat.

And the worst part is that *all these have been experienced and reported by astronauts who went out and returned.*

71. We are all mutants. And that is a good thing.

There are three mechanisms which power the evolution of life – those are *mutations, natural selection,* and *genetic drift.* By biological definition, a *mutation* is a trait which is not inherited from parents (or grandparents, or great-grandparents, and so on), but a completely new piece of genetic information which did not occur before. Subsequently, a *mutant* is by definition an organism which has at least one mutation – opposite of a *clone.*

However, mutations occur in virtually every single newborn organism – be it a microorganism, a plant, an animal, and of course – a human being. In fact, statistics have shown that *every human being bears around a hundred mutations* – which is more than two mutations per chromosome.

This is *both* scary – because it can sometimes cause anomalies in our bodies – and a good thing – because it has, through history of life, shown to be beneficial, giving new generations of organisms a better chance to adapt to the ever-changing environment.

72.   *We are a suicidal species.*

Humans are a unique species for many things, and one of them is an extremely high suicide rate. While most animals and plants never even ponder such a deed, even among those who do, cases are few and far in between.

On the other hand, according to the World Health Organization, *one person takes their life every 40 seconds*. This is a worldwide statistic. Take out your stopwatch and measure 40 seconds. By the time you do, statistics say that *someone, somewhere, has committed suicide.* Try to imagine how many will do so by the time you finish reading this book.

73.   *High suicide rates – in detail*

Guayana, South America is the country with the highest suicide rate. There was even a death cult which performed a mass murder-suicide of *no less than 909* people. That happened in 1978, but even nowadays the suicide rate is almost 45 on every 100,000 people. The next are both North and South Korea, with North Korea being substantially above South (almost 40 vs. under 30 suicides on every 100,000 people).

Japan is an interesting country here, too. Their own news claim that their suicide rates – although much lower than those mentioned above – are not as high as reported. In fact, they supposedly *report suicides in order to mask unsolved murder crimes.*

74. Growing fingernails and noses after death?

Here is another well-known myth, with the truth being a little bit more disturbing. We all probably heard this story – after you die, your hair, nails and nose continue growing for a few hours (some claim even days).

The truth is, they do not. What really happens is that your skin and the fat underneath it starts *shrinking*, which makes some peripherals – mainly hair, nails and nose – perceived as slightly longer. The hair is pushed out a little bit due to tissue shrinkage, while nails have a constant length which becomes relatively larger after the skin shrinks. Similar happens to the nose, which features a sharp gristle underneath its tip. The gristle keeps your nose at the same length, while the facial skin and fat shrinks.

When we think about it, it is all perfectly logical – once we die, game over. There is no more growth or development – which is the main point of death.

75. What if we cannot afford a funeral?

This is a question most people will evade in everyday talk, due to the topic being not as jolly as most other. However, there is a reported number of over half a million homeless people in the USA only. In 2005, the worldwide estimated number was as high as 100 million, while another billion lacked "adequate housing" (meaning they are – theoretically – just a bit better off than homeless). So where do those people go when they die?

In New York City, USA, there is a solution for this. Hart Island, a place which was closed to the public for 35 years, is likely the largest mass graveyard in the USA. *An estimated million homeless people are buried there,* in mass graves which hold up to 50 adults or 1,000 children. *The graves are maintained by prisoners* of the New York Metropolitan Correctional Center.

76.   Two men, one heart – one widow?!

It was over the news around the end of 2010s – a man called Sonny Graham, 57 at the time, had received a heart transplantation which saved his life. The heart had belonged to Terry Cottle, an adopted father of two, and a husband of a woman named Cheryl, who had taken his life at the age of 33.

Here is where things got creepy. Mr. Graham suddenly changed some of his life habits, including his food and drink preferences, which now strangely matched Mr. Cottle's. On top of that – he fell in love with Cheryl, Mr. Cottle's widow. Soon after, they married.

However, there was no happy ending to this story. 13 years later, Sonny Graham, who had previously never displayed any signs of mental or emotional instability, *took his life as well – in much the same way* as late mr. Cottle did.

So who says our brain is our only thing responsible for our thoughts and emotions?

77.   *Living severed heads*

Until 1977, France still used guillotines (originally called Louisettes, having little to do with Dr. Guillotin), which provides us with fairly up-to-date reports. The method was deemed "humane" and fairly "painless", bearing the idea that there was little sense in torturing a criminal sentenced to death. This may be the reason why the crowd got quickly bored with this execution method.

However, reports throughout history, both recent and older, witness that after decapitation, the head is still "alive" for a few moments. There are numerous documents and rumors which claim that the severed head, after being triumphantly lifted by the executioner, made several facial expressions – from nondescript grimaces and twitches, to eye blinks and even tongues sticking out!

Whether those were involuntary reflexes of a still partially functioning nerve system, or the "last breaths" of a brain which had a little bit of energy left in it after decapitation is still unknown, and will probably remain so for some time now. And for the better, we should say...

78.   *Are we human, or bacteria?*

The human body, on average, consists of over one hundred trillion cells. That's 1 with *fourteen* zeroes, or 10 to the power of 14 (10^{14}). However, less than 40 trillion of it are actually *human* cells –

everything else is bacteria. Yes, we are still talking about a healthy human body.

As it turns out, we are more bacteria than we are human. This may sound overly dramatic, and when put in context, it actually is. The factual state is that we *need* all those bacteria as much as they need us to survive – in biology, this phenomena is known as *symbiosis*, and is known to have existed in evolution of life even before actual multicellular organisms were around. Still, it is a somewhat terrifying thought – especially nowadays when we are surrounded by all those "anti-bacterial products".

79. *How much dust is dead human skin?*

We have encountered this factoid a number of times – supposedly, 80% of dust around us are tiny pieces of dead human skin. Gross, is it not? Too gross to be true, in fact – the whole story is a **hoax**. Unless, of course, you are an ever-molting bird or a reptile, who *never* happens to open your house doors or windows. Every time you do, however, the in-house dust is stirred and mixed with airborne dust from outside. This kind of dust are tiny dirt, soil and inorganic materials.

While we do shed a lot of our dead skin, it stays pretty close to our bodies until we take our clothes off and have a good shower. So all that "gross" stuff gets washed down our sewers – but it does leave a question open, how much of our dead body bits is drained down there?

80. We decompose our own dead bodies

Remember the fact we mentioned about our bodies hosting trillions of bacteria earlier? It is about to get weirder any moment now.

No more than three days (72 hours) after a human body dies, the still-living bacteria continue their work. And now that there is no living immune system to prevent them from doing whatever they please, they start to run amok. It starts with the bacteria living in our digestive tracts, which start releasing enzymes that decompose our bodies. There is a wealth of food for them here, too – especially since they can digest just about anything organic.

These bacteria and enzymes will spread through our entire body and slowly eat us up, after the process called *autolysis* is finished.

81. Humans multiply very quickly.

Alright, we know we do. But just *how* quickly? The numbers are borderline scary here. It is a known fact that nowadays the *human population is more than all the people who ever lived in the past.*

There is a classic school riddle about amoebas. Let us assume we have a petri dish containing a single amoeba. The amoeba multiplies by two every second. If after 30 seconds the petri dish is half-full of amoeba, how long will it take until it is completely full? While many people will say 60 seconds (forgetting the multiplication by two), the right answer is 31 second.

Human population is similar, to an extent. By the end of 2010s, there were nearly four births each second worldwide, against only two deaths. By 2015, these numbers have *slightly* raised – in favor of births.

82.   *There is no such thing as dying of old age.*

Strangely enough, there is no age limit hard-coded within our genes. As medicine progresses, average life expectancy of humans grows. Statistics also show that in countries which have better, more sophisticated medical care, the population grows older than in countries where they do not.

However, during our lifetime, we are likely to catch various diseases and other health problems, most of which leave a lasting effect on our bodies. As those gather up, our chances of survival approach zero.

Another cause of death is lack of certain hormones – such as serotonin – which are produced at decreasing rates as we age. Once some of those reach zero, we die. Here is the crazy part, however – such causes of death are the least common ones.

83.   *We do not have the same number of bones through our lives.*

As we grow, some bones change, and then at a later age, there is a multitude of diseases that can affect the shape and size of our bones. But *our bones also drastically change in number*.

Evidently, babies are born with 270 bones in their bodies. We all do, unless there was some unexpected mutation or anomaly. By the time we grow up, however, *the number of our bones reduces to 206. This is a shrinkage of over 30%.*

So where do the bones go? Essentially, they *fuse together* as we grow. For example, a newborn's skull consists of five pieces which later "stitch" together. Similar is true for shoulders, ribs and the pelvis. This allows the baby to easier exit the mother's womb when being born, and later does wonders to prevent fractures, until we learn how to walk.

84. The fearsome number 13

It is both astonishing and downright creepy how many people fall prone to the superstitions regarding this simple prime number.

While haunted houses are doing great business on any given Friday 13th, since this theme is neither as common or as predictable as, e.g. Halloween, statistics have shown that celebrations like weddings are surprisingly scarce on such a date, *some agencies reporting no less than 50% less people* choosing that particular day to get married. Real estate agents are losing here as well – *over 40% people refuse to buy a house that is addressed at number 13*. The air fares at some travel agencies are the cheapest on Friday 13th as well – people steer clear of flying on that date so much, that *some prices fall down to 30% of their original value* – losing no less than $800 million on that day in 2015.

85. The gruesome fairy-tales

We have probably all heard stories about Snow White, The Little Red Riding Hood, The Little Mermaid, and so on. And we all know they are classic folk-tales which found their way into contemporary era – and a lot of cartoons and feature films. But what did they look like originally? Well...

The Little Mermaid has no happy ending at all. The charming

prince married the witch in disguise, which made the mermaid we all love so sad that *she instantly died*. And that just relieved her off the pain she was enduring until then.

Snow White was probably the least changed – at least it has a happy ending for the protagonist. On the other hand, *the witch died in torture and agony that makes the Spanish Inquisition look like a kindergarten.*

Sleeping Beauty did not fall asleep at all. *She died instead of falling asleep, the prince raped her and her dead body gave birth to twins,* before one of the children revives her.

Goldilocks was mauled and eaten by the three bears. Enough said.

And The Little Red Riding hood was in fact a voluptuous young woman on her way to Grandma's house. There was no grandma, though, nor the lumberjack father/uncle at the end of the journey. *Just the wolf who ate her, having her given false directions previously.*

It's somewhat a good thing that we have "modernized" versions of these fairy-tales, so we do not give our children nightmares before bedtime.

86.   *Al Bundy and Jay Pritchett are slow readers.*

There is little doubt in the cultural impact which the series "Married... with Children" did, along with its main actor, Ed O'Neill, who somewhat repeats the role in the series "Modern Family."

In both series, the main protagonist, played by Mr. O'Neill can be seen reading newspapers, on multiple occasions. Between over 20 years through which both series were aired (the first started on 1987, the second in 2009), there were multiple occasions of the protagonist reading *exactly the same piece of newspaper.*

As it turns out, the paper was printed by Earl Hays Press, one of the greatest newspaper prop companies in the USA. The same paper has seen more than those two series – it appeared in "Desperate Housewives", "Everybody Hates Chris", "Scrubs", and a similar one appeared in "The Sopranos", as well as "No Country for Old Men."

87.   *Watching horror films makes you lose weight.*

A study was conducted at the University of Westminster which observed vital acitivities of volunteers who were given various horror movies to watch – from "The Texas Chainsaw Massacre" to "Paranormal Activity", along with other genres of film, such as romance and sitcoms.

The study was mostly focused on monitoring the volunteers' heart rates, but also included sweat levels, breathing rate, and eventually the energy consumption of the body. As it turns out, while watching horror films, *the volunteers burned a substantial amount of calories,* whereas the activity during other films it was barely measurable.

Stanley Kubrick's film "The Shining" has shown to burn the most – nearly a whopping 200 calories during the film, which equals to an hour-long walk outside. The runner-ups were "Jaws" and "The Exorcist", which burned roughly 160 and 150 calories, respectively.

88.   The fearsome Gary Oldman

Gary Oldman is arguably one of the best contemporary Hollywood actors. One of his planetary successes was the portrayal of the legendary Dracula in Francis Ford Coppola's 1992 film "Bram Stoker's Dracula".

There was a scene in the said film, where Dracula shape-shifts into a bat, which mr. Oldman did not consider to be *scary enough*. Thus, he personally went from one actor to another, and whispered something in their ears – after which their expressions of horror were terrifyingly genuine.

Nobody knows what were the exact words which mr. Oldman whispered.

89.   The picky Stanley Kubrick

Stanley Kubrick was an iconic film director, whose films nowadays enjoy either cult or classic statuses – or both. He was known to both terrify people as well as make them think, on numerous levels.

For his cult-classic film "The Shining", an adaptation of Stephen King's novel of the same name, he chose Jack Nicholson to play the leading role. However, there were other choices available before him.

Robert De Niro was one of the potential actors, but Kubrick thought *he was not psychotic enough* for the role. We can see how, being guided by that thought, he chose Nicholson instead.

Another candidate was refused – Robin Williams. For him, Kubrick thought *he was too psychotic*. Imagine that.

90. *Carl Sagan approves!*

Once known worldwide as one of the most popular and most competent astronomers, Carl Sagan was somewhat of a modern "Renaissance man", whose interests included film as well. He was an advisor on Stanley Kubrick's project "2001: A Space Odyssey", among others, in order to make the science fiction film as plausible as possible.

However, beside his knowledge on astrophysics (and film), his voice was also heard in other fields, from philosophy to quantum physics. When asked about time travel, can you guess which was his favorite?

It was no less than Robert Zemeckis' "Back to the Future Part II". Sagan argued that *the film very accurately described parallel timelines*.

Good to know there was at least one person in the 20th century who understood the concept well enough.

91. *Alice Cooper is a good swinger*

Alice Cooper is a famous rock star, and was once deemed "the scariest man in the world". After decades of musical and visual success, it is rather difficult to imagine him singing a ballad, let alone appear in public without shocking everyone around. Black (or punk-like) clothing, a good amount of make-up, as well as costumes and iconography he uses are guaranteed to give goosebumps to those who see him for the first time.

Unless, of course, he is swinging a golf club. Yes, golf – Alice Cooper is an avid player, who claims to usually play golf five or six times a week. He even claims it was golf which helped him get rid of his alcohol addiction.

Now try to imagine him in that version. We are no longer sure which one is scarier.

92.   Collective nouns

We all know about a *flock of birds*, a *bouquet of flowers* and a *herd of cows*. There is also an *army of soldiers*, a *class of students* and a *crowd of people*. But did you know there are many other nouns in the English language which have their respective collections called in a fun way?

There is a *business of ferrets*, a *bob of seals* and a *zeal of zebras*. There is also an *eloquence of lawyers*, a *board of directors*, and a *balance of accountants*. And a collective of crows is called a *murder*. Quite appropriate, is it not?

93.   The not-so-graceful career starts

We all know of great blockbuster films and their alleged stars, but how did they manage to get there in the first place? While it is clear that their intelligence and charms are above average, they should have started *somewhere*, right?

Sylvester stallone begun his career in 1970s, featuring in a "soft" adult film called "The Italian Stallion". Jackie Chan's road started roughly at the same time, in a Hong Kong film of such genre. So did Cameron Diaz, although her own such film was "homemade". On the other hand, Arnold Schwarzenegger started as a photo model in a gay erotic magazine. The famous Marilyn Monroe, previously known as Norma Jean, started her career by "wearing" only some perfume for the Playboy magazine.

The following is a small collection of gathered urban myths and legends which have either proven to be true, or hold at least *some* ground in actual events.

94. The Mountain Pass of Death

There is a mountain in the Ural range in Russia, called the Kholat Syakhl Mountain (aka the Mountain of the Dead). There, in February 1959, a mysterious and tragic incident occurred, which sparked interest and speculation for decades.

Nine ski-hikers had disappeared there at the beginning of the month, only to be found some time later, all dead. The shroud of mystery that covered this case was composed of the following facts – some of them were completely naked, some had fatal fractures on their bodies, there was a substantial amount of radiation found in their clothes – and *one of them was missing their tongue.*

Although the mystery is still not completely solved, it was later found out that they all died of hypothermia. The fact that some of them were naked was because the *extreme cold had fried their cold receptors, making them feel as if they were actually too hot.* The missing tongue was credited to a wild animal – most likely a bear – which came to feast on the fresh meat, while *the fractures were most likely due to a fall after losing conscience due to the cold.* The radiation, however, was identified as one coming from a K-40 isotope, primarily used in laboratories.

The incident sparked a number of conspiracy theories, which only added to its fame.

95. The first woman to fly over the Atlantic Ocean

If you look up any relevant history book, the name Amelia Mary Earhart will pop up. She is well-known among historians and aviation enthusiasts – and her fame is well-deserved. Among the numerous feats she performed was flying over the Atlantic Ocean – not only as the first woman who did so, but also for doing it *on her own*. That's right – no copilots, no assistance of any kind. Solo.

She disappeared at the age of 39. A year and a half later, she was proclaimed dead *in absentia* (aka missing in action). However, despite a good number of evidence (along with recordings and transcripts of her radio transmissions), quite a few different speculations have emerged by now. Therefore, *there is no consensus under which circumstances her life had ended.*

96. Mysterious disappearances of people

The case of Amelia Mary Earhart above is, sadly, not a solitary one at all. Just since the year 2000, there are records of over 60 people only in the USA who went missing. Some of those people are so far declared "legally dead", but *the bodies were never found*, let alone were the circumstances regarding their disappearance ever solved.

Such is the case of Brandon Swanson, who was last seen in May 2008, at age 19. The search for him is still out, as long as the officials have the approval of his family. The initial search for him covered 122 square miles (over 315 km²), since Swanson had the ability to walk a very long distance on his own. On top of that, *no evidence of criminal activity was ever found*, nor was there any evidence that Swanson had merely staged his own disappearance.

Another example is a musician Derek Serpell-Moris, also known as DJ Derek, "Britain's oldest DJ", who went missing in 2015, *at the age of 74.* There is also no found evidence of crime here, and there are indications that he could have not gone abroad.

97. *Horror rolled in a carpet*

Never take random discarded stuff off the streets.

In 1984, three Columbia University students were returning to their dorm, when they found a discarded, rolled-up carpet. Not being very well off, they decided it would be a good idea to take the carpet home and decorate their room with it.

The carpet felt strangely heavy, so all three had to carry it – *only to discover a dead body inside, once* they unrolled it in their dorm. It was a murder victim, an African-American male in his 20s who had been shot to the head. *It was never identified.*

98. A patient emitting toxic gas

In February 1994, Gloria Ramirez, 31, was taken into ER in Riverside, California. She was dying of cervical cancer, and was half-awake at best. Attempts to communicate with her yielded limited results, the woman mostly giving brief and incoherent answers. Standard procedure included taking a blood sample. But when the sample was taken, the nurse felt a smell of chemicals in the young woman's blood.

This is where chaos started. No less than 23 staff members who were in contact with the patient have shown various symptoms of intoxication by the said chemicals, which were fuming out of the woman's blood. They had felt lightheaded, lost consciousness, and eventually, after waking up, had little to no control over their limbs. Gloria Ramirez died due to kidney failure.

There is no clear consensus over what exactly happened there. Investigators attempted to explain the strange course of events in a number of occasions, with very limited results. The badly decomposed body of Gloria Ramirez was buried in an unmarked grave. Eventually, the case grew to be a basis for an episode of *X-Files*, the popular paranormal mystery series around the turning of the 21st century.

99. Human torches

No, this is not about a comic-book superhero. There have been dozens of reports of people suddenly – and somewhat mysteriously

– bursting into flames and thus dying a burning, painful death. Between the 18th and 19th century, it was recognized as a genuine concern among citizens of the Western world. The fear of it was additionally fueled – no pun intended – by popular authors like Mark Twain and Charles Dickens writing about such events. The victim of such an accident would suddenly, seemingly without any cause, be set aflame and burn out, *while damaging little to no of their surroundings.*

The scary part is, *some of those reports were actually true.* Although the explanations for them are not as mysterious or paranormal as we might expect, it *can* happen. And sometimes, just sometimes, it *does.* Despite our bodies being between composed of 60% – 70% non-flammable water, our clothes are not. On top of that, when dehydrated and heavily intoxicated by flammable substances, such as alcohol, in proximity of small flames (matches, cigarettes, et al.), the body can indeed be set afire.

A medical condition exists, called the *Stevens-Johnson syndrome*, a skin disease in which a patient can sometimes, especially post-mortem, be mistaken for a burnt victim of the spontaneous human combustion.

And in the end – although science is yet to find any compelling evidence for or against "human torches", occasionally a case emerges in the news, where *no other explanation can be provided at any time.*

100. The Paris cannibal

Issei Sagawa is a Japanese man, who in 1981 *made Hannibal Lecter look like a gentleman.* His was one of the most gruesome and tragic recent cases of cannibalism in the Western world, committed in June 1981, in Paris. Nine years prior to that, he was charged in Tokyo, Japan, for an attempted rape. What he admitted only later was, it was also an attempt of cannibalism.

However, Renée Hartevelt, a beautiful and healthy young Dutch girl studying in Paris was not as lucky. Sagawa invited her to his apartment, before shooting her and cutting her body up with a butcher's knife. After having spent two days eating the young woman's flesh, he was caught trying to dump her remains.

The worst part of this case follows. After two years of being trialed in France, he was able to walk away under the pledge of insanity. Since then, *he lives in Japan as a free man and a minor celebrity.*

101. Real-life vampires

Some crimes can only be described as vampiric in nature, although no actual blood-sucking was involved. Instead, the truth turned out to be a little bit more disturbing.

During 2010s in Peru, South America, a series of evidence was exposed which caught *a gang of serial killers, which gathered their victims' fat.* The story was connected to a vampire legend that circled around South America for four centuries, and was charged for killing roughly *50 murders each year.*

The affair was met with skepticism, especially from the experts, who rightfully claim that human fat is virtually worthless, especially since *liposuction surgery clinics dump tons of such grease on a weekly basis*. This, however, leaves the question unanswered – where did all this gathered human fat go?

THE END

www.ingramcontent.com/pod-product-compliance
Lightning Source LLC
Chambersburg PA
CBHW062059280526
45788CB00003B/1284